POEMS

by Rainer Maria Rilke

TO THE MEMORY OF
AUGUSTE RODIN
THROUGH WHOM I CAME TO KNOW
RAINER MARIA RILKE

Start Publishing PD LLC
Copyright © 2024 by Start Publishing PD LLC

All rights reserved, including the right to reproduce this book or portions thereof in any form whatsoever.

Start Publishing PD is a registered trademark of Start Publishing PD LLC
Manufactured in the United States of America

Cover art: Shutterstock/Taisiya Kozorez

Cover design: Jennifer Do

10 9 8 7 6 5 4 3 2 1

ISBN 979-8-8809-1001-4

POEMS

by Rainer Maria Rilke
Translated by Jessie Lamont

Contents

Introduction: The Poetry of Rainer Maria Rilke

First Poems
Evening 22
Mary Virgin 23

The Book of Pictures
Presaging 24
Autumn 25
Silent Hour 26
The Angels 27
Solitude 28
Kings in Legends 29
The Knight 30
The Boy 31
Initiation 32
The Neighbour 33
Song of the Statue 34
Maidens I 35
Maidens II 36
The Bride 37
Autumnal Day 38
Moonlight Night 39
In April 40
Memories of a Childhood 41
Death 42
The Ashantee 43

Remembrance	44
Music	45
Maiden Melancholy	46
Maidens at Confirmation	47
The Woman who Loves	49
Pont du Carrousel	50
Madness	51
Lament	52
Symbols	53

New Poems

Early Apollo	54
The Tomb of a Young Girl	55
The Poet	56
The Panther	57
Growing Blind	58
The Spanish Dancer	59
Offering	60
Love Song	61
Archaic Torso of Apollo	62

The Book of Hours

The Book of a Monk's Life	63
I Live my Life in Circles	63
Many have Painted Her	64
In Cassocks Clad	65
Thou Anxious One	66
I Love My Life's Dark Hours	67

The Book of Pilgrimage

By Day Thou are the Legend and the Dream	68

All Those Who Seek Thee 69
In a House Was One 70
Extinguish My Eyes. 71
In the Deep Nights 72

The Book of Poverty and Death

Her Mouth 73
Alone Thou Wanderest 74
A Watcher of Thy Spaces 75

Introduction: The Poetry of Rainer Maria Rilke

The supreme problem of every age is that of finding its consummate artistic expression. Before this problem every other remains of secondary importance. History defines and directs its physical course, science cooperates in the achievement of its material aims, but Art alone gives to the age its spiritual physiognomy, its ultimate and lasting expression.

The process of Art is on the one hand sensuous, the conception having for its basis the fineness of organization of the senses; and on the other hand it is severely scientific, the value of the creation being dependent upon the craftsmanship, the mastery over the tool, the technique.

Art, like Nature, its great and only reservoir for all time past and all time to come, ever strives for elimination and selection. It is severe and aristocratic in the application of its laws and impervious to appeal to serve other than its own aims. Its purpose is the symbolization of Life. In its sanctum there reigns the silence of vast accomplishment, the serene, final, and imperturbable solitude which is the ultimate criterion of all great things created.

To speak of Poetry is to speak of the most subtle, the most delicate, and the most accurate instrument by which to measure Life.

Poetry is reality's essence visioned and made manifest by one endowed with a perception acutely sensitive to sound, form, and colour, and gifted with a power to shape into rhythmic and rhymed verbal symbols the reaction to Life's phenomena. The poet moulds that which appears evanescent and ephemeral in image and in mood into everlasting values. In this act of creation he serves eternity.

Poetry, in especial lyrical poetry, must be acknowledged the supreme art, culminating as it does in a union of the other arts, the musical, the plastic, and the pictorial.

The most eminent contemporary poets of Europe have, each in accordance with his individual temperament, reflected in their work the spiritual essence of our age, its fears and failures, its hopes and high achievements: Maeterlinck, with his mood of resignation and his retirement into a dusky twilight where his shadowy figures move noiselessly like phantoms in fate-laden dimness; Dehmel, the worshipper of will, with his passion for materiality and the beauty of all things physical and tangible; Verhaeren, the visionary of a new vitality, who sees in the toilers of fields and factories the heroic gesture of our time and who might have written its great epic of industry but for the overwhelming lyrical mood of his soul.

Until a few years ago, known only to a relatively small community on the continent but commanding an ever increasing attention which has borne his name far beyond the boundary of his country, the personality of Rainer Maria Rilke stands to-day beside the most illustrious poets of modern Europe.

The background against which the figure of Rainer Maria Rilke is silhouetted is so varied, the influences which have entered into his life are so manifold, that a study of his work, however slight, must needs take into consideration the elements through which this poet has matured into a great master.

Prague, the city in which Rilke was born in 1875, with its sinister palaces and crumbling towers that rose in the early Middle Ages and have reached out into our time like the threatening fingers of mighty hands which have wielded swords for generations and which are stained with the blood of many wounds of many races; the city where amid grey old ruins blonde maidens are at play or are lost in reverie in the green cool parks and shady gardens with which the Bohemian capital abounds, this Prague of mingled grotesqueness and beauty gave to the young boy his first impressions.

There is a period in the life of every artist when his whole being seems lost in a contemplation of the surrounding world, when the application to work is difficult, like the violent forcing of something that is awaiting its time. This is the time of his dream, as sacred as the days of early spring before wind and rain and light have touched the fruits of the fields, when there is a tense bleak silence over the whole of nature, in which is wrapped the strength of storms and the glow of the summer's sun. This is the time of his deepest dream, and upon this dream and its guarding depends the final realization of his life's work.

The young graduate of the Gymnasium was to enter upon the career of an army officer in accordance with the traditions of the family, an old noble house which traces its lineage far back to Carinthian ancestry. His inclinations, however, pointed so decisively in the direction of the finer arts of life that he left the Military Academy after a very short attendance to devote himself to the study of philosophy and the history of art.

As one turns the pages of Rilke's first small book of poems, published originally under the title *Larenopfer*, in the year 1895, and which appeared in more recent editions under the less descriptive name *Erste Gedichte*, one realizes at once, in spite of a lack of plasticity in the presentation, that here speaks one who has lingered long and lovingly over the dream of his boyhood. As the title indicates, these poems are a tribute, an offering to the Lares, the home spirits of his native town. Prague and the surrounding country are the ever recurring theme of almost every one of these poems. The meadows, the maidens, the dark river in the evening, the spires of the cathedral at night rising like grey mists are seen with a wonderment, the great well-spring of all poetic imagination, with a well-nigh religious piety. Through all these poems there sounds like a subdued accompaniment a note of gratitude for the ability to thus vision the world, to be sunk in the music of all things. "Without is everything that I feel within myself, and without and within myself everything is immeasurable, illimitable."

These pictures of town and landscape are never separated from their personal relation to the poet. He feels too keenly his dependence upon them, as a child views flowers and stars as personal possessions. Not until later was he to reach the height of an impersonal objectivity in his art. What distinguishes these early poems from similar adolescent productions is the restraint in the presentation, the economy and intensity of expression and that quality of listening to the inner voice of things which renders the poet the seer of mankind.

The second book of poems appeared two years later and like the first volume *Traumgekrönt* is full of the music that is reminiscent of the mild melancholy of the Bohemian folk-songs, in whose gentle rhythms the barbaric strength of the race seems to be lulled to rest as the waves of a far-away tumultuous sea gently lap the shore. The themes of *Traumgekrönt* are extended somewhat beyond the immediate environment of Prague and some of the most beautiful poems are luminous pictures of villages hidden in the snowy blossoming of May and June, out of which rises here and there the solitary soft voice of a boy or girl singing. In these first two volumes the poet is satisfied with painting in words, full of sonorous beauty, the surrounding world. From this period dates the small poem *Evening*, which seems to have been sketched by a Japanese painter, so clear and colourful is its texture, so precious and precise are its outlines.

With *Advent* and *Mir Zur Feier*, both published within the following three years, a phase of questioning commences, a dim desire begins to stir to reach out into the larger world "deep into life, out beyond time." Whereas the early poems were characterized by a tendency to turn away from the turmoil of life—in fact, the concrete world of reality does not seem to exist—there is noticeable in these two later volumes an advance toward life in the sense that the poet is beginning to approach and to vision some of its greatest symbols.

Throughout the entire work of Rilke, in his poetry as well as in his interpretations of painting and sculpture, there are two elements that constitute the cornerstones in the structure of his art. If, as has been said with a degree of verity, Nietzsche was primarily a musician whose philosophy had for its basis and took its ultimate aspects from the musical quality of his artistic endowment, it may be maintained with an equal amount of truth that Rilke is primarily a painter and sculptor whose poetry rests upon the fundaments of the pictorial and plastic arts.

Up to the time of the publication of these volumes, Rilke's poems possessed a quietude, a stillness suggested in the straight unbroken yet delicate lines of the picture which he portrays and in the soft, almost unpulsating rhythm of his words. The approach of evening or nightfall, the coming of dawn, the change of the seasons, the slow changes of light into darkness and of darkness into light, in short, the most silent yet greatest metamorphoses in the external aspects of nature form the contents of many of these first poems. The inanimate object and the living creature in nature are not seen in the sharp contours of their isolation; they are viewed and interpreted in the atmosphere that surrounds them, in which they are enwrapped and so densely veiled that the outlines are only dimly visible, be that atmosphere the mystic grey of northern twilight or the dark velvety blue of southern summer nights. In *Advent*, the experience of the atmosphere becomes an experience in his innermost soul and, therefore, all things become of value to him only in so far as they partake of the atmosphere, as they are seen in a peculiar air and distance. This first phase in Rilke's work may be defined as the phase of reposeful nature.

To this sphere of relaxation and restfulness in which the objects are static and are changed only as the surrounding atmosphere affects them, the second phase in the poet's development adds another element, which later was to grow into dimensions so powerful, so violently breaking beyond the limitations of simple expression in words that it could only find its satisfaction in a dithyrambic hymn to the work of the great plastic artist of our time, to the creations of Auguste Rodin. This second element is that which the French sculptor in a different medium has carried to perfection. It is the element of gesture, of dramatic movement.

This might seem the appropriate place in which to speak of Rilke's monograph on the art of Rodin. To do so would, however, be an undue anticipation, for it will be necessary to trace Rilke's development through several transitions before the value of his contact with the work of Rodin can be fully measured.

The gesture, the movement begins in *Advent* and *Celebration* to disturb the stillness prevailing in the first two volumes of poems. Even here it is only gentle and shy at first like the stirring of a breath of wind over a quiet sea;

and gentle beings make this first gesture, children and young women at play, singing, dancing or at prayer.

Particularly in the cycle *Songs of the Maidens* in the book *Celebration*, the atmosphere is condensed and becomes the psychic background of the landscape against which the gesture of longing or expectation is seen and felt. It is the impatience to burst into blossoming, the longing for love which pulsates in these *Songs of the Maidens* with the tenseness of suspense. *The Prayers of the Maidens to Mary* have not the mild melody of maidenly prayer; they vibrate with the ecstasy of expectant life, and the Madonna is more than the Heavenly Virgin, their longing transforms her into the symbol of earthly love and motherhood. This expectation, in spite of its intensity, is subdued and is only heard like the cadence of a far off dream:

"How shall I go on tiptoe
From childhood to Annunciation
Through the dim twilight
Into Thy Garden?"

Mention should be made of some prose writings which Rilke published in the year 1898 and shortly afterward. They are *Two Stories of Prague*, *The Touch of Life* and *The Last*; three volumes of short stories; a two-act drama, *The Daily Life*, points to a strong Maeterlinck influence, and finally *Stories of God*. With both beauty of detail and problematic interest, the short stories show an incoherence of treatment and a lack of dramatic co-ordination easily conceivable in a poet who is essentially lyrical and who at that time had not mastered the means of technique to give to his characters the clear chiselling of the epic form.

A sojourn in Russia and especially the acquaintance with the novels of Dostoievsky became potent factors in Rilke's development and served to deepen creations which without this influence might have terminated in a grandiose æsthesia.

Broadly speaking, Russian art and literature may be described as springing from an ethical impulse and as having for their motive power and *raison d'être* the tendency toward socio-political reform, in contradistinction to the art and literature of Western culture, whose motives and aims are primarily of an æsthetic nature and seek in art the reconciliation of the dualism between spirit and matter.

Dostoievsky, whom Merejkovsky describes somewhere as the man with the never-young face, the face "with its shadows of suffering and its wrinkles of sunken-in cheeks ... but that which gives to this face its most tortured expression is its seeming immobility, the suddenly interrupted impulse, the life hardened into a stone:" this Dostoievsky and particularly his *Rodion Raskolnikov* cycle became a profound artistic experience to Rilke. The poor, the outcasts, the homeless ones received for him a new significance, the significance of the isolated figure placed in the mighty everchanging current of a life in which this figure stands strong and solitary. In the poem entitled *Pont Du Carrousel*, written in Paris a few years later, Rilke has visioned the blind beggar aloof amid the fluctuating crowds of the metropolis.

Of Russia and its influence upon him, Rilke writes: "Russia became for me the reality and the deep daily realization that reality is something that comes infinitely slowly to those who have patience. Russia is the country where men are solitary, each one with a world within himself, each one profound in his humbleness and without fear of humiliating himself, and because of that truly pious. Here the words of men are only fragile bridges above their real life."

The great symbols of Solitude and of Death enter into the poet's work.

In the first decade of the new century Rilke reached the height of his art and with a few exceptions the poems represented in this volume are selected from the poems which were published between the years 1900 and 1908. The ascent toward the acme of Rilke's art after the year 1900 is as rapid as it is precipitous. Only a few years previous we read in Advent:

"That is longing: To dwell in the flux of things,

To have no home in the present.

POEMS

And these are wishes: gentle dialogues
Of the poor hours with eternity."

With *Das Buch der Bilder* the dream is ended, the veil of mist is lifted and before us are revealed pictures and images that rise before our eyes in clear colourful contours. Whether the poet conjures from the depths of myth *The Kings in Legends*, or whether we read from *The Chronicle of a Monk* the awe-inspiring description of *The Last Judgment Day*, or whether in Paris on a Palm Sunday we see *The Maidens at Confirmation*, the pictures presented stand out with the clearness and finality of the typical.

It is a significant fact that Rilke dedicated this book to Gerhart Hauptmann, "in love and gratitude for his Michael Kramer." Hauptmann, like Rilke in these poems, has placed before us great epic figures and his art is so concentrated that often the simple expression of the thought of one of his characters produces a shudder in the listener or reader because in this thought there vibrates the suffering of an entire social class and in it resounds the sorrow of many generations.

In *The Book of Pictures*, Rilke's art reaches its culmination on what might be termed its monumental side. The visualization is elevated to the impersonal objective level which gives to the rhythm of these poems an imperturbable calm, to the figures presented a monumental erectness. *The Men of the House of Colonna, The Czars, Charles XII Riding Through the Ukraine* are portrayed each with his individual historical gesture, with a luminosity as strong as the colour and movement which they gave to their time. In the mythical poem, *Kings in Legends*, this concrete element in the art of Rilke has found perhaps its supreme expression:

"Kings in old legends seem
Like mountains rising in the evening light.
They blind all with their gleam,
Their loins encircled are by girdles bright,
Their robes are edged with bands
Of precious stones—the rarest earth affords—

With richly jeweled hands
They hold their slender, shining, naked swords."

There are in *The Book of Pictures* poems in which this will to concentrate a mood into its essence and finality is applied to purely lyrical poems as in *Initiation*, that stands out in this volume like "the great dark tree" itself so immeasurable is the straight line of its aspiration reaching into the far distant silence of the night; or as in the poem entitled *Autumn*, with its melancholy mood of gentle descent in all nature.

In *The Book of Hours*, Rilke withdraws from the world not from weariness but weighed down under the manifold conflicting visions. As the prophet who would bring to the world a great possession must go forth into the desert to be alone until the kingdom comes to him from within, so the poet must leave the world in order to gain the deeper understanding, to be face to face with God. The mood of *Das Stunden-Buch* is this mood of being face to face with God; it elevates these poems to prayer, profound prayer of doubt and despair, exalted prayer of reconciliation and triumph.

The Book of Hours contains three parts written at different periods in the poet's life: *The Book of a Monk's Life* (1899); *The Book of Pilgrimage* (1901), and *The Book of Poverty and Death* (1903), although the entire volume was not published until several years later. *The Book of Hours* glows with a mystic fervour to know God, to be near him. In this desire to approach the Nameless One, the young Brother in *The Book of a Monk's Life* builds up about God parables, images and legends reminiscent of those of the 17th century Angelus Silesius, but sustained by a more pregnant language because exalted by a more ardent visionary force. The motif of *The Monk's Life* is expressed in the poem beginning with the lines:

"I live my life in circles that grow wide
And endlessly unroll."

Through the grey cell of the young Monk there flash in luminous magnificence the colours of the great renaissance masters, for he feels in Titian, in Michelangelo, in Raphael the same fervour that animates him; they, too, are worshippers of the same God.

POEMS

There are poems in *The Book of Pilgrimage* of the stillness of a whispered prayer in a great Cathedral and there are others that carry in their exultation the music of mighty hymns. The visions in this second book are no less ecstatic though less glowingly colourful; they have withdrawn inward and have brought a great peace and a great faith as in the poem of God, whose very manifestation is the quietude and hush of a silent world:

"By day Thou art the Legend and the Dream
That like a whisper floats about all men,
The deep and brooding stillnesses which seem,
After the hour has struck, to close again.
And when the day with drowsy gesture bends
And sinks to sleep beneath the evening skies,
As from each roof a tower of smoke ascends
So does Thy Realm, my God, around me rise."

The last part of *The Book of Hours*, *The Book of Poverty and Death*, is finally a symphony of variations on the two great symbolic themes in the work of Rilke. As Christ in the parable of the rich young man demands the abandonment of all treasures, so in this book the poet sees the coming of the Kingdom, the fulfilment of all our longings for a nearness to God when we have become simple again like little children and poor in possessions like God Himself. In this phase of Rilke's development, the principle of renunciation constitutes a certain negative element in his philosophy. The poet later proceeded to a positive acquiescence toward man's possessions, at least those acquired or created in the domain of art.

In our approach through the mystic we touch reality most deeply. It is because of this that all art and all philosophy culminate in their final forms in a crystallization of those values of life that remain forever inexplicable to pure reason; they become religious in the simple, profound sense of that word. Before the eternal facts of Life doubt and strife are reconciled into faith, will and pride change into humility. The realization of this truth expressed in the medium of poetry is the significance of Rilke's *Book of Hours*. A distinguished Scandinavian writer has pronounced *Das Stunden-Buch* one of the supreme literary achievements of our time and its deepest and most beautiful book of prayer.

In his subsequent poetic work Rilke did not again reach the sustained high quality of this book, the mood and idea of which he incorporated into a prose work of exquisite lyrical beauty: *The Sketch of Malte Laurids Brigge.*

In *New Poems* (1907) and *New Poems, Second Part* (1908) the historical figure, frequently taken from the Old Testament, has grown beyond the proportions of life; it is weightier with fate and invariably becomes the means of expressing symbolically an abstract thought or a great human destiny. *Abishag* presents the contrast between the dawning and the fading life; *David Singing Before Saul* shows the impatience of awakening ambition, and *Joshua* is the man who forces even God to do his will. The antique Hellenic world rises with shining splendour in the poems *Eranna to Sappho, Lament for Antinous, Early Apollo* and the *Archaic Torso of Apollo.*

The spirit of the Middle Ages with its religious fervour and superstitious fanaticism is symbolized in several poems, the most important among which are *The Cathedral, God in the Middle Ages, Saint Sebastian* personifying martyrdom, and *The Rose Window,* whose glowing magic is compared to the hypnotic power of the tiger's eye. Modern Paris is often the background of the *New Poems,* and the crass play of light and shadow upon the waxen masks of Life's disillusioned in the Morgue is caught with the same intense realistic vision as the flamingos and parrots spreading their vari-coloured soft plumage in the warmth of the sun in the Avenue of the Jardin des Plantes.

Almost all of the poems in these two volumes are short and precise. The images are portrayed with the sensitive intensity of impressionistic technique. The majestic quietude of the long lines of *The Book of Pictures* is broken, the colours are more vibrant, more scintillating and the pictures are painted in nervous, darting strokes as though to convey the manner in which they were perceived: in one single, all-absorbing glance. For this reason many of these *New Poems* are not quite free from a certain element of virtuosity. On the other hand, Rilke achieves at times a perfect surety of rapid stroke as in the poem *The Spanish Dancer*, who rises luminously on the horizon of our inner vision like a circling element of fire, flaming and blinding in the momentum of her movements. Degas and Zuloaga seem to have combined their art on one canvas to give to this dancer the abundant elasticity of grace and the splendid fantasy of colour.

Many of the themes in the *New Poems* bear testimony to the fact that Rilke travelled extensively, prior to the writing of these volumes, in Italy, Germany, France, and Scandinavia. His book on the five painters at the artists' colony at Worpswede, where he remained for a time, entirely given over to the observation of the atmosphere, the movement of the sky and the play of light upon the far heath of this northern landscape, is an introduction to every interpretation of the work of landscape painters and a tender poem to a land whose solitary and melancholy beauty entered into his own work.

More vital than the influence of the personalities and the art treasures of the countries which Rilke visited and more potent in its effect upon his creations, like a great sun over the most fruitful years of his life, stands the towering personality of Auguste Rodin. The *New Poems* bear the dedication: "A mon grand ami, Auguste Rodin," indicating the twofold influence which the French sculptor wielded over the poet, that of a friend and that of an artist.

One recalls the broad, solidly-built figure of Rodin with his rugged features and high, finely chiselled forehead, moving slowly among the white glistening marble busts and statues as a giant in an old legend moves among the rocks and mountains of his realm, patient, all-enduring, the man who has mastered life, strong and tempered by the storms of time. And one thinks of Rainer Maria Rilke, young, blond, with his slender aristocratic figure, the slightly bent-forward figure of one who on solitary walks meditates much and intensely, with his sensitive full mouth and the "firm structure of the eyebrow gladly sunk in the shadow of contemplation," the face full of dreams and with an expression of listening to some distant music.

From no other book of his, not excepting *The Book of Hours*, can we deduce so accurate a conception of Rilke's philosophy of Life and Art as we can draw from his comparatively short monograph on Auguste Rodin.

Rilke sees in Rodin the dominant personification in our age of the "power of servitude in all nature." For this reason the book on Rodin is far more than a purely æsthetic valuation of the sculptor's work; Rilke traces throughout the book the strongly ethical principle which works itself out in every creative act in the realm of art. This grasp of the deeper significance of all art gives to the book on Rodin its well-nigh religious aspect of thought and its hymnlike rhythm of expression. He begins: "Rodin was solitary before fame came to him, and afterward he became perhaps still more solitary. For fame is ultimately but the summary of all misunderstandings that crystallize about a new name." And he sums up this one man's greatness: "Sometime it will be realized what has made this great artist so supreme. He was a worker whose only desire was to penetrate with all his forces into the humble and the difficult significance of his tool. Therein lay a certain renunciation of life but in just this renunciation lay his triumph—for Life entered into his work."

Rodin became to Rilke the manifestation of the divine principle of the creative impulse in man. Thus Rilke's monograph on Auguste Rodin will remain the poet's testament on Life and Art.

Rilke has lived deeply; he has absorbed into his artistic and spiritual consciousness many of the supreme values of our time. His art holds the mystic depth of the Slav, the musical strength of the German, and the visual clarity of the Latin. As artist, he has felt life to be sacred, and as a priest, he has brought to its altar many offerings.

H.T.
NEW YORK CITY,
AUTUMN, 1918.

FIRST POEMS

EVENING

The bleak fields are asleep,
My heart alone wakes;
The evening in the harbour
Down his red sails takes.

Night, guardian of dreams,
Now wanders through the land;
The moon, a lily white,
Blossoms within her hand.

RAINER MARIA RILKE

MARY VIRGIN

How came, how came from out thy night
Mary, so much light
And so much gloom:
Who was thy bridegroom?

Thou callest, thou callest and thou hast forgot
That thou the same art not
Who came to me
In thy Virginity.

I am still so blossoming, so young.
   How shall I go on tiptoe
   From childhood to Annunciation
   Through the dim twilight
   Into thy Garden.

THE BOOK OF PICTURES

PRESAGING

I am like a flag unfurled in space,
I scent the oncoming winds and must bend with them,
While the things beneath are not yet stirring,
While doors close gently and there is silence in the chimneys
And the windows do not yet tremble and the dust is still heavy—
Then I feel the storm and am vibrant like the sea
And expand and withdraw into myself
And thrust myself forth and am alone in the great storm.

RAINER MARIA RILKE

AUTUMN

The leaves fall, fall as from far,
Like distant gardens withered in the heavens;
They fall with slow and lingering descent.

And in the nights the heavy Earth, too, falls
From out the stars into the Solitude.

Thus all doth fall. This hand of mine must fall
And lo! the other one:—it is the law.
But there is One who holds this falling
Infinitely softly in His hands.

POEMS

SILENT HOUR

Whoever weeps somewhere out in the world
Weeps without cause in the world
Weeps over me.

Whoever laughs somewhere out in the night
Laughs without cause in the night
Laughs at me.

Whoever wanders somewhere in the world
Wanders in vain in the world
Wanders to me.

Whoever dies somewhere in the world
Dies without cause in the world
Looks at me.

RAINER MARIA RILKE

THE ANGELS

They all have tired mouths
And luminous, illimitable souls;
And a longing (as if for sin)
Trembles at times through their dreams.

They all resemble one another,
In God's garden they are silent
Like many, many intervals
In His mighty melody.

But when they spread their wings
They awaken the winds
That stir as though God
With His far-reaching master hands
Turned the pages of the dark book of Beginning.

POEMS

SOLITUDE

Solitude is like a rain
That from the sea at dusk begins to rise;
It floats remote across the far-off plain
Upward into its dwelling-place, the skies,
Then o'er the town it slowly sinks again.
Like rain it softly falls at that dim hour
When ghostly lanes turn toward the shadowy morn;
When bodies weighed with satiate passion's power
Sad, disappointed from each other turn;
When men with quiet hatred burning deep
Together in a common bed must sleep—
Through the gray, phantom shadows of the dawn
Lo! Solitude floats down the river wan …

RAINER MARIA RILKE

KINGS IN LEGENDS

Kings in old legends seem
Like mountains rising in the evening light.
They blind all with their gleam,
Their loins encircled are by girdles bright,
Their robes are edged with bands
Of precious stones—the rarest earth affords—
With richly jeweled hands
They hold their slender, shining, naked swords.

POEMS

THE KNIGHT

The Knight rides forth in coat of mail
Into the roar of the world.
And here is Life: the vines in the vale
And friend and foe, and the feast in the hall,
And May and the maid, and the glen and the grail;
God's flags afloat on every wall
In a thousand streets unfurled.

Beneath the armour of the Knight
Behind the chain's black links
Death crouches and thinks and thinks:
"When will the sword's blade sharp and bright
Forth from the scabbard spring
And cut the network of the cloak
Enmeshing me ring on ring—
When will the foe's delivering stroke
Set me free
To dance
And sing?"

RAINER MARIA RILKE

THE BOY

I wish I might become like one of these
Who, in the night on horses wild astride,
With torches flaming out like loosened hair
On to the chase through the great swift wind ride.
I wish to stand as on a boat and dare
The sweeping storm, mighty, like flag unrolled
In darkness but with helmet made of gold
That shimmers restlessly. And in a row,
Behind me in the dark, ten men that glow
With helmets that are restless, too, like mine,
Now old and dull, now clear as glass they shine.
One stands by me and blows a blast apace
On his great flashing trumpet and the sound
Shrieks through the vast black solitude around
Through which, as through a wild mad dream we race.
The houses fall behind us on their knees,
Before us bend the streets and them we gain,
The great squares yieled to us and them we seize—
And on our steeds rush like the roar of rain.

POEMS

INITIATION

Whosoever thou art! Out in the evening roam,
Out from thy room thou know'st in every part,
And far in the dim distance leave thy home,
Whosoever thou art.
Lift thine eyes which lingering see
The shadows on the foot-worn threshold fall,
Lift thine eyes slowly to the great dark tree
That stands against heaven, solitary, tall,
And thou hast visioned Life, its meanings rise
Like words that in the silence clearer grow;
As they unfold before thy will to know
Gently withdraw thine eyes—

RAINER MARIA RILKE

THE NEIGHBOUR

Strange violin! Dost thou follow me?
In many foreign cities, far away,
Thy lone voice spoke to me like memory.
Do hundreds play thee, or does but one play?

Are there in all great cities tempest-tossed
Men who would seek the rivers but for thee,

Who, but for thee, would be forever lost?
Why drifts thy lonely voice always to me?
Why am I the neighbour always
Of those who force to sing thy trembling strings?
Life is more heavy—thy song says—
Than the vast, heavy burden of all things.

POEMS

SONG OF THE STATUE

Who so loveth me that he
Will give his precious life for me?
I shall be set free from the stone
If some one drowns for me in the sea,
I shall have life, life of my own,—
For life I ache.

I long for the singing blood,
The stone is so still and cold.
I dream of life, life is good.
Will no one love me and be bold
And me awake?

. . . .

I weep and weep alone,
Weep always for my stone.
What joy is my blood to me
If it ripens like red wine?
It cannot call back from the sea
The life that was given for mine,
Given for Love's sake.

RAINER MARIA RILKE

MAIDENS I

Others must by a long dark way
Stray to the mystic bards,
Or ask some one who has heard them sing
Or touch the magic chords.
Only the maidens question not
The bridges that lead to Dream;
Their luminous smiles are like strands of pearls
On a silver vase agleam.

The maidens' doors of Life lead out
Where the song of the poet soars,
And out beyond to the great world—
To the world beyond the doors.

POEMS

MAIDENS II

Maidens the poets learn from you to tell
How solitary and remote you are,
As night is lighted by one high bright star
They draw light from the distance where you dwell.

For poet you must always maiden be
Even though his eyes the woman in you wake
Wedding brocade your fragile wrists would break,
Mysterious, elusive, from him flee.

Within his garden let him wait alone
Where benches stand expectant in the shade
Within the chamber where the lyre was played
Where he received you as the eternal One.

Go! It grows dark—your voice and form no more
His senses seek; he now no longer sees
A white robe fluttering under dark beech trees
Along the pathway where it gleamed before.

He loves the long paths where no footfalls ring,
And he loves much the silent chamber where
Like a soft whisper through the quiet air
He hears your voice, far distant, vanishing.

The softly stealing echo comes again
From crowds of men whom, wearily, he shuns;
And many see you there—so his thought runs—
And tenderest memories are pierced with pain.

THE BRIDE

Call me, Beloved! Call aloud to me!
Thy bride her vigil at the window keeps;
The evening wanes to dusk, the dimness creeps
Down empty alleys of the old plane-tree.

O! Let thy voice enfold me close about,
Or from this dark house, lonely and remote,
Through deep blue gardens where gray shadows float
I will pour forth my soul with hands stretched out ...

POEMS

AUTUMNAL DAY

Lord! It is time. So great was Summer's glow:
Thy shadows lay upon the dials' faces
And o'er wide spaces let thy tempests blow.

Command to ripen the last fruits of thine,
Give to them two more burning days and press
The last sweetness into the heavy wine.

He who has now no house will ne'er build one,
Who is alone will now remain alone;
He will awake, will read, will letters write
Through the long day and in the lonely night;
And restless, solitary, he will rove
Where the leaves rustle, wind-blown, in the grove.

RAINER MARIA RILKE

MOONLIGHT NIGHT

South-German night! the ripe moon hangs above
Weaving enchantment o'er the shadowy lea.
From the old tower the hours fall heavily
Into the dark as though into the sea—
A rustle, a call of night-watch in the grove,
Then for a while void silence fills the air;
And then a violin (from God knows where)
Awakes and slowly sings: Oh Love ... Oh Love ...

POEMS

IN APRIL

Again the woods are odorous, the lark
Lifts on upsoaring wings the heaven gray
That hung above the tree-tops, veiled and dark,
Where branches bare disclosed the empty day.

After long rainy afternoons an hour
Comes with its shafts of golden light and flings
Them at the windows in a radiant shower,
And rain drops beat the panes like timorous wings.

Then all is still. The stones are crooned to sleep
By the soft sound of rain that slowly dies;
And cradled in the branches, hidden deep
In each bright bud, a slumbering silence lies.

MEMORIES OF A CHILDHOOD

The darkness hung like richness in the room
When like a dream the mother entered there
And then a glass's tinkle stirred the air
Near where a boy sat in the silent gloom.

The room betrayed the mother—so she felt—
She kissed her boy and questioned "Are you here?"
And with a gesture that he held most dear
Down for a moment by his side she knelt.

Toward the piano they both shyly glanced
For she would sing to him on many a night,
And the child seated in the fading light
Would listen strangely as if half entranced,

His large eyes fastened with a quiet glow
Upon the hand which by her ring seemed bent
And slowly wandering o'er the white keys went
Moving as though against a drift of snow.

POEMS

DEATH

Before us great Death stands
Our fate held close within his quiet hands.
When with proud joy we lift Life's red wine
To drink deep of the mystic shining cup
And ecstasy through all our being leaps—
Death bows his head and weeps.

RAINER MARIA RILKE

THE ASHANTEE

(Jardin d'Acclimatation, Paris)

No vision of exotic southern countries,
No dancing women, supple, brown and tall
Whirling from out their falling draperies
To melodies that beat a fierce mad call;

No sound of songs that from the hot blood rise,
   No langorous, stretching, dusky, velvet maids
   Flashing like gleaming weapon their bright eyes,
   No swift, wild thrill the quickening blood pervades.

Only mouths widening with a still broad smile
Of comprehension, a strange knowing leer
At white men, at their vanity and guile,
An understanding that fills one with fear.

The beasts in cages much more loyal are,
Restlessly pacing, pacing to and fro,
Dreaming of countries beckoning from afar,
Lands where they roamed in days of long ago.

They burn with an unquenched and smothered fire
Consumed by longings over which they brood,
Oblivious of time, without desire,
Alone and lost in their great solitude.

POEMS

REMEMBRANCE

Expectant and waiting you muse
On the great rare thing which alone
To enhance your life you would choose:
The awakening of the stone,
The deeps where yourself you would lose.

In the dusk of the shelves, embossed
Shine the volumes in gold and browns,
And you think of countries once crossed,
Of pictures, of shimmering gowns
Of the women that you have lost.

And it comes to you then at last—
And you rise for you are aware
Of a year in the far off past
With its wonder and fear and prayer.

RAINER MARIA RILKE

MUSIC

What play you, O Boy? Through the garden it stole
Like wandering steps, like a whisper—then mute;
What play you, O Boy? Lo! your gypsying soul
Is caught and held fast in the pipes of Pan's flute.

And what conjure you? Imprisoned is the song,
It lingers and longs in the reeds where it lies;
Your young life is strong, but how much more strong
Is the longing that through your music sighs.

Let your flute be still and your soul float through
Waves of sound formless as waves of the sea,
For here your song lived and it wisely grew
Before it was forced into melody.

Its wings beat gently, its note no more calls,
Its flight has been spent by you, dreaming Boy!
Now it no longer steals over my walls—
But in my garden I'd woo it to joy.

POEMS

MAIDEN MELANCHOLY

A young knight comes into my mind
As from some myth of old.

He came! You felt yourself entwined
As a great storm would round you wind.
He went! A blessing undefined
Seemed left, as when church-bells declined
And left you wrapt in prayer.
You fain would cry aloud—but bind
Your scarf about you and tear-blind
Weep softly in its fold.

A young knight comes into my mind
Full armored forth to fare.

His smile was luminously kind
Like glint of ivory enshrined,
Like a home longing undivined,
Like Christmas snows where dark ways wind,
Like sea-pearls about turquoise twined,
Like moonlight silver when combined
With a loved book's rare gold.

RAINER MARIA RILKE

MAIDENS AT CONFIRMATION

(Paris in May, 1903)

The white veiled maids to confirmation go
Through deep green garden paths they slowly wind;
Their childhood they are leaving now behind:
The future will be different, they know.

Oh! Will it come? They wait—It must come soon!
The next long hour slowly strikes at last,
The whole house stirs again, the feast is past,
And sadly passes by the afternoon ...

Like resurrection were the garments white
The wreathed procession walked through trees arched wide
Into the church, as cool as silk inside,
With long aisles of tall candles flaming bright:
The lights all shone like jewels rich and rare
To solemn eyes that watched them gleam and flare.

Then through the silence the great song rose high
Up to the vaulted dome like clouds it soared,
Then luminously, gently down it poured—
Over white veils like rain it seemed to die.

The wind through the white garments softly stirred
And they grew vari-coloured in each fold

POEMS

And each fold hidden blossoms seemed to hold
And flowers and stars and fluting notes of bird,
And dim, quaint figures shimmering like gold
Seemed to come forth from distant myths of old.

Outside the day was one of green and blue,
With touches of a luminous glowing red,
Across the quiet pond the small waves sped.
Beyond the city, gardens hidden from view
Sent odors of sweet blossoms on the breeze
And singing sounded through the far off trees.

It was as though garlands crowned everything
And all things were touched softly by the sun;
And many windows opened one by one
And the light trembled on them glistening.

RAINER MARIA RILKE

THE WOMAN WHO LOVES

Ah yes! I long for you. To you I glide
And lose myself—for to you I belong.
The hope that hitherto I have denied
Imperious comes to me as from your side
Serious, unfaltering and swift and strong.

Those times: the times when I was quite alone
By memories wrapt that whispered to me low,
My silence was the quiet of a stone
Over which rippling murmuring waters flow.

But in these weeks of the awakening Spring
Something within me has been freed—something
That in the past dark years unconscious lay,
Which rises now within me and commands
And gives my poor warm life into your hands
Who know not what I was that Yesterday.

POEMS

PONT DU CARROUSEL

Upon the bridge the blind man stands alone,
Gray like a mist veiled monument he towers
As though of nameless realms the boundary stone
About which circle distant starry hours.

He seems the center around which stars glow
While all earth's ostentations surge below.

Immovably and silently he stands
Placed where the confused current ebbs and flows;
Past fathomless dark depths that he commands
A shallow generation drifting goes....

MADNESS

She thinks: I am—Have you not seen?
Who are you then, Marie?
I am a Queen, I am a Queen!
To your knee, to your knee!

And then she weeps: I was—a child—
Who were you then, Marie?
Know you that I was no man's child,
Poor and in rags—said she.

And then a Princess I became
To whom men bend their knees;
To princes things are not the same
As those a beggar sees.

And those things which have made you great
Came to you, tell me, when?
One night, one night, one night quite late,
Things became different then.

I walked the lane which presently
With strung chords seemed to bend;
Then Marie became Melody
And danced from end to end.

The people watched with startled mien
And passed with frightened glance
For all know that only a Queen
May dance in the lanes: dance!...

POEMS

LAMENT

Oh! All things are long passed away and far.
A light is shining but the distant star
From which it still comes to me has been dead
A thousand years ... In the dim phantom boat
That glided past some ghastly thing was said.
A clock just struck within some house remote.
Which house?—I long to still my beating heart.
Beneath the sky's vast dome I long to pray ...
Of all the stars there must be far away
A single star which still exists apart.
And I believe that I should know the one
Which has alone endured and which alone
Like a white City that all space commands
At the ray's end in the high heaven stands.

RAINER MARIA RILKE

SYMBOLS

From infinite longings finite deeds rise
As fountains spring toward far-off glowing skies,
But rushing swiftly upward weakly bend
And trembling from their lack of power descend—
So through the falling torrent of our fears
Our joyous force leaps like these dancing tears.

NEW POEMS

EARLY APOLLO

As when at times there breaks through branches bare
A morning vibrant with the breath of spring,
About this poet-head a splendour rare
Transforms it almost to a mortal thing.

There is as yet no shadow in his glance,
　Too cool his temples for the laurel's glow;
　But later o'er those marble brows, perchance,
　A rose-garden with bushes tall will grow,

　And single petals one by one will fall
　O'er the still mouth and break its silent thrall,
　—The mouth that trembles with a dawning smile
　As though a song were rising there the while.

THE TOMB OF A YOUNG GIRL

We still remember! The same as of yore
All that has happened once again must be.
As grows a lemon-tree upon the shore—
It was like that—your light, small breasts you bore,
And his blood's current coursed like the wild sea.

That god—
who was the wanderer, the slim
Despoiler of fair women; he—the wise,—
But sweet and glowing as your thoughts of him
Who cast a shadow over your young limb
While bending like your arched brows o'er your eyes.

POEMS

THE POET

You Hour! From me you ever take your flight,
Your swift wings wound me as they whir along;
   Without you void would be my day and night,
   Without you I'll not capture my great song.

I have no earthly spot where I can live,
I have no love, I have no household fane,
And all the things to which myself I give
Impoverish me with richness they attain.

THE PANTHER

His weary glance, from passing by the bars,
Has grown into a dazed and vacant stare;
It seems to him there are a thousand bars
And out beyond those bars the empty air.

The pad of his strong feet, that ceaseless sound
Of supple tread behind the iron bands,
Is like a dance of strength circling around,
While in the circle, stunned, a great will stands.

But there are times the pupils of his eyes
Dilate, the strong limbs stand alert, apart,
Tense with the flood of visions that arise
Only to sink and die within his heart.

POEMS

GROWING BLIND

Among all the others there sat a guest
   Who sipped her tea as if one apart,
   And she held her cup not quite like the rest;
   Once she smiled so it pierced one's heart.

   When the group of people arose at last
   And laughed and talked in a merry tone,
   As lingeringly through the rooms they passed
   I saw that she followed alone.

   Tense and still like one who to sing must rise
   Before a throng on a festal night
   She lifted her head, and her bright glad eyes
   Were like pools which reflected light.

   She followed on slowly after the last
   As though some object must be passed by,
   And yet as if were it once but passed
   She would no longer walk but fly.

RAINER MARIA RILKE

THE SPANISH DANCER

As a lit match first flickers in the hands
Before it flames, and darts out from all sides
Bright, twitching tongues, so, ringed by growing bands
Of spectators—she, quivering, glowing stands
Poised tensely for the dance—then forward glides

And suddenly becomes a flaming torch.
Her bright hair flames, her burning glances scorch,
And with a daring art at her command
Her whole robe blazes like a fire-brand
From which is stretched each naked arm, awake,
Gleaming and rattling like a frightened snake.

And then, as though the fire fainter grows,
She gathers up the flame—again it glows,
As with proud gesture and imperious air
She flings it to the earth; and it lies there
Furiously flickering and crackling still—
Then haughtily victorious, but with sweet
Swift smile of greeting, she puts forth her will
And stamps the flames out with her small firm feet.

POEMS

OFFERING

My body glows in every vein and blooms
To fullest flower since I first knew thee,
My walk unconscious pride and power assumes;
Who art thou then—thou who awaitest me?

When from the past I draw myself the while
I lose old traits as leaves of autumn fall;
I only know the radiance of thy smile,
Like the soft gleam of stars, transforming all.

Through childhood's years I wandered unaware
Of shimmering visions my thoughts now arrests
To offer thee, as on an altar fair
That's lighted by the bright flame of thy hair
And wreathèd by the blossoms of thy breasts.

RAINER MARIA RILKE

LOVE SONG

When my soul touches yours a great chord sings!
How shall I tune it then to other things?
O! That some spot in darkness could be found
That does not vibrate whene'er your depths sound.
But everything that touches you and me
Welds us as played strings sound one melody.
Where is the instrument whence the sounds flow?
And whose the master-hand that holds the bow?
O! Sweet song—

POEMS

ARCHAIC TORSO OF APOLLO

   We cannot fathom his mysterious head,
   Through the veiled eyes no flickering ray is sent:
   But from his torso gleaming light is shed
   As from a candelabrum; inward bent
   His glance there glows and lingers. Otherwise
   The round breast would not blind you with its grace,
   Nor could the soft-curved circle of the thighs
   Steal to the arc whence issues a new race.
   Nor could this stark and stunted stone display
   Vibrance beneath the shoulders heavy bar,
   Nor shine like fur upon a beast of prey,
   Nor break forth from its lines like a great star—
There is no spot that does not bind you fast
   And transport you back, back to a far past.

THE BOOK OF HOURS

The Book of A Monk's Life

I live my life in circles that grow wide
And endlessly unroll,
I may not reach the last, but on I glide
Strong pinioned toward my goal.

About the old tower, dark against the sky,
The beat of my wings hums,
I circle about God, sweep far and high
On through milleniums.

Am I a bird that skims the clouds along,
Or am I a wild storm, or a great song?

POEMS

Many have painted her. But there was one
Who drew his radiant colours from the sun.
Mysteriously glowing through a background dim
When he was suffering she came to him,
And all the heavy pain within his heart
Rose in his hands and stole into his art.
His canvas is the beautiful bright veil
Through which her sorrow shines. There where the
Texture o'er her sad lips is closely drawn
A trembling smile softly begins to dawn ...
Though angels with seven candles light the place
You cannot read the secret of her face.

RAINER MARIA RILKE

In cassocks clad I have had many brothers
In southern cloisters where the laurel grows,
They paint Madonnas like fair human mothers
And I dream of young Titians and of others
In which the God with shining radiance glows.

But though my vigil constantly I keep
My God is dark—like woven texture flowing,
A hundred drinking roots, all intertwined;
I only know that from His warmth I'm growing.
More I know not: my roots lie hidden deep
My branches only are swayed by the wind.

POEMS

Thou Anxious One! And dost thou then not hear
Against thee all my surging senses sing?
About thy face in circles drawing near
My thought floats like a fluttering white wing.

Dost thou not see, before thee stands my soul
In silence wrapt my Springtime's prayer to pray?
But when thy glance rests on me then my whole
Being quickens and blooms like trees in May.

When thou art dreaming then I am thy Dream,
But when thou art awake I am thy Will
Potent with splendour, radiant and sublime,
Expanding like far space star-lit and still
Into the distant mystic realm of Time.

I love my life's dark hours
In which my senses quicken and grow deep,
While, as from faint incense of faded flowers
Or letters old, I magically steep
Myself in days gone by: again I give
Myself unto the past:—again I live.

Out of my dark hours wisdom dawns apace,
Infinite Life unrolls its boundless space ...

Then I am shaken as a sweeping storm
Shakes a ripe tree that grows above a grave
'Round whose cold clay the roots twine fast and warm—
And Youth's fair visions that glowed bright and brave,
Dreams that were closely cherished and for long,
Are lost once more in sadness and in song.

THE BOOK OF PILGRIMAGE

By day Thou are the Legend and the Dream
   That like a whisper floats about all men,
   The deep and brooding stillnesses which seem,
   After the hour has struck, to close again.

   And when the day with drowsy gesture bends
   And sinks to sleep beneath the evening skies,
   As from each roof a tower of smoke ascends—
   So does Thy Realm, my God, around me rise.

RAINER MARIA RILKE

All those who seek Thee tempt Thee,
And those who find would bind Thee
To gesture and to form.

But I would comprehend Thee
As the wide Earth unfolds Thee.
Thou growest with my maturity,
Thou Art in calm and storm.

I ask of Thee no vanity
To evidence and prove Thee.
Thou Wert in eons old.

Perform no miracles for me,
But justify Thy laws to me
Which, as the years pass by me.
All soundlessly unfold.

POEMS

In a house was one who arose from the feast
And went forth to wander in distant lands,
Because there was somewhere far off in the East
A spot which he sought where a great Church stands.
And ever his children, when breaking their bread,
Thought of him and rose up and blessed him as dead.

In another house was the one who had died,
Who still sat at table and drank from the glass
And ever within the walls did abide—
For out of the house he could no more pass.
And his children set forth to seek for the spot
Where stands the great Church which he forgot.

Extinguish my eyes, I still can see you,
Close my ears, I can hear your footsteps fall,
And without feet I still can follow you,
And without voice I still can to you call.
Break off my arms, and I can embrace you,
Enfold you with my heart as with a hand.
Hold my heart, my brain will take fire of you
As flax ignites from a lit fire-brand—
And flame will sweep in a swift rushing flood
Through all the singing currents of my blood.

POEMS

In the deep nights I dig for you, O Treasure!
To seek you over the wide world I roam,
For all abundance is but meager measure
Of your bright beauty which is yet to come.

Over the road to you the leaves are blowing,
Few follow it, the way is long and steep.
You dwell in solitude—Oh, does your glowing
Heart in some far off valley lie asleep?

My bloody hands, with digging bruised, I've lifted,
Spread like a tree I stretch them in the air
To find you before day to night has drifted;
I reach out into space to seek you there ...

Then, as though with a swift impatient gesture,
Flashing from distant stars on sweeping wing,
You come, and over earth a magic vesture
Steals gently as the rain falls in the spring.

THE BOOK OF POVERTY AND DEATH

Her mouth is like the mouth of a fine bust
That cannot utter sound, nor breathe, nor kiss,
But that had once from Life received all this
Which shaped its subtle curves, and ever must
From fullness of past knowledge dwell alone,
A thing apart, a parable in stone.

POEMS

    Alone Thou wanderest through space,
Profound One with the hidden face;
      Thou art Poverty's great rose,
      The eternal metamorphose
      Of gold into the light of sun.

    Thou art the mystic homeless One;
    Into the world Thou never came,
    Too mighty Thou, too great to name;
    Voice of the storm, Song that the wild wind sings,
    Thou Harp that shatters those who play Thy strings!

A watcher of Thy spaces make me,
Make me a listener at Thy stone,
Give to me vision and then wake me
Upon Thy oceans all alone.
Thy rivers' courses let me follow
Where they leap the crags in their flight
And where at dusk in caverns hollow
They croon to music of the night.
Send me far into Thy barren land
Where the snow clouds the wild wind drives,
Where monasteries like gray shrouds stand—
August symbols of unlived lives.
There pilgrims climb slowly one by one,
And behind them a blind man goes:
With him I will walk till day is done
Up the pathway that no one knows …

www.ingramcontent.com/pod-product-compliance
Lightning Source LLC
Chambersburg PA
CBHW031418040426
42444CB00005B/635